CALLUM MORTON MORE TALK ABOUT BUILDINGS AND MOOD

DIRECTOR'S FOREWORD

Callum Morton: More Talk about Buildings and Mood is the eleventh in an ongoing series of solo exhibitions by leading Australian artists on Level 4 of the MCA. With a focus on Morton's architectural models from the past four years, the exhibition highlights his strategy of injecting wry humour and cinematic drama into iconic architecture, critiquing its Utopian intentions.

Since the early 1990s Morton has been constructing architectural fragments and models and producing richly coloured digital images that bring together 'high' and 'low' architecture. The tension between theory and practice, art and life is examined through the ways that architects design our social environment and how people actually utilise buildings. This slippage provides a rich source of material for Morton, who animates his models with sound and light to create vivid narratives of human frailty.

Since the opening of its Level 4 galleries in 1999, the MCA has profiled in depth the work of a number of major Australian artists. Artists who have exhibited their work in this series include Guan Wei, Dale Frank, Mikala Dwyer, Kathleen Petyarre, Lyndal Jones, Hossein Valamanesh, Patricia Piccinini, Dorothy Napangardi, Maria Fernanda Cardoso, and Susan Norrie. Other Level 4 initiatives include the pairing of Australian artists with their international peers, which has seen projects realised by Ricky Swallow with Texan sculptor Erick Swenson, and Mathew Jones with British artist Simon Starling.

The MCA Ambassadors support the Museum's Level 4 projects, and we are indebted to them for their generous nurturing of Australian contemporary art. We thank Callum Morton for his time and care in developing this exhibition, including the creation of two major new works; the exhibition's curator, Stuart Koop, for his work on the exhibition and catalogue; catalogue contributor Philip Brophy; and the artist's representatives in Australia, Anna Schwartz in Melbourne and Roslyn Oxley in Sydney. Thanks also go to all the lenders to the exhibition.

Elizabeth Ann Macgregor
Director Museum of Contemporary Art

THE STORY OF ARCHITECTURE

Callum Morton was born the day Le Corbusier died. You may also read that Morton briefly studied architecture before dropping out and studying art. Or that his father was an architect, in fact, that he worked with Moshe Safdie on the original Habitat building in Montreal, to which Morton has recently referred in his work. All of these things are helpful in understanding the artist's critical relationship to architecture: as an Oedipal drama; as an avant-garde succession; and as a generation gap.

For the past decade Callum Morton has been building architectural models and fragments that set familiar forms from architectural history against their original, idealised purpose and this contest has been staged at the threshold between inside and outside. First, bringing the outside inside, the fragments drawn into the gallery from outlying streets: awnings, balconies, brick walls, windows, timber panels, all reproduced at three quarter scale. Then, whole buildings, rebuilt in the manner of architectural models, and animated in contrary ways with strange sounds and lights such that what goes

on inside spills out into the space beyond. Like the Farnsworth House, designed by Mies van der Rohe in 1945. It appears in Morton's work on several occasions, not as a well-preserved icon of Modernist design, but with the addition of sound and lights, as the incidental site of suburban drama and mayhem. In one model, a wild party rages within, ending with gunshots and screams, possibly a murder. In another model, the House is duplicated and arranged to form a compound or court, wherein we can see and hear the occupants of one house watching a horror movie on television, while others are throwing a party, while their neighbours are getting burgled. In these works, less is not more as Mies

Above: *Mixed Business*
(from the series *Been There*) 1998-99
Wood, steel, acrylic paint
15 x 150 x 50 cm
Private collection
Image courtesy the artist and
Roslyn Oxley9 Gallery, Sydney
Photo: The artist

suggested, nor does form follow function, as Louis Sullivan said it should. But architecture becomes a stage or proscenium for various events set within and against it.

In other works by Morton, Philip Johnson's Glass House from 1949 is recast as an abandoned gas station in the middle of nowhere; or Adalberto Libera's Casa Malaparte, built on a dramatic promontory of rock jutting into the Mediterranean, emits a single phrase enunciated robotically over and over *ad absurdum*: 'Silenzio'. Morton has also picked some curios from the Modernist canon, like the holiday cabin where Le Corbusier died of a heart attack, wherein we see and hear the grand master flatline, or Melbourne's own Gas and Fuel buildings, which were destroyed to make way for the new, much vaunted Federation Square.

In this endeavour, Morton appears to be an iconoclast, ultimately critical of the Utopian ideals that these remarkable buildings embody, undermining their seriousness with dramatic and often

humorous narratives drawn from life or from movies or from books or from his own experience. The ideal world composed by architects is filled with grisly ends and grimy details: death, S&M, conflict, loss, annulment. Thus he renders an alternative, corrupted architectural history, and the pristine, empty, quasi-sacred spaces of the world's renowned buildings are filled to bursting with all sorts of profane events.

Indeed, architecture is often separated from its real history, from the specific and actual circumstances surrounding the production of its iconic forms, which suggests an underside to the annals or cannon, perhaps even an unconscious: the return of what has been repressed in any merely formal account of developments. Writing about architecture 'from the outside', Elizabeth Grosz accounts for this 'excess' in theoretical terms borrowed from George Bataille and Luce Irigaray. On the one hand, she proposes that which exceeds proper or good taste, 'for Bataille, dirt, disorder, contagion, expenditure, filth, immoderation and – above all – shit',

and on the other a 'maternal-feminine ground', as it turns out, the very concept of space, which is systematised and divided up in architectural discourse and practice. The excess is then both the precondition for the imposition of order or cleanliness, and that which is intolerable to it. [1]

To put it another simpler way, Edith Farnsworth had to keep her garbage in a closet down the hall for twenty years until she sold the house in 1975, because of Mies's strict edict on transparency, which included windows even beneath the sink; 'you can see the whole "kitchen" from the road', Edith complained. And so while critics

describe the House in terms of floating, planar forms, set amongst the gorgeousness of a grassy meadow on the bank of the Fox River in Illinois, Edith writes in her memoirs of feeling more like 'a prowling animal' kept within a glass cage for all to see. [2] For Mies didn't declare the interior of the building to his client until it was built, and she never asked about it. His pencil sketches refused much detail and opaque panels were used in the model to indicate glass. Even after viewing the model at New York's Museum of Modern Art in 1947, Edith Farnsworth wrote how happy she was to be involved in a project 'that might well become the prototype of new and important elements of American

architecture'. [3] But by 1951, she felt a 'dupe' and 'victim' of the architect, and rumours of her romance with Mies quickly dissipated in a lawsuit over costs and an open brawl in the press.

In Morton's model, *International Style 1999*, we can hear a woman's plaintive voice; 'Don't you dare touch me' she screams, before firing off five rounds. It's evidently a specific reference to the client/architect relationship, kept in the margins of the official or architect's story of the House, and only subsequently revealed in expositions undertaken by critical, and feminist, historians like Alice T. Friedman or Beatriz Colomina (dabbling in what Colomina calls 'the messy space of archive' [4]). As Grosz argues, 'femininity' is repeatedly revealed as 'that which the architectural cannot contain within its own drives to orderliness and systematicity'. [5]

But conflicts in these models are also generic. Although distilled from real events, they clearly refer to all our lives, since we all fall in and out of love, we all have fights and break up, crimes of

passion are commonplace. In this sense, the events are typical. And it's no surprise either that outrage and bitterness, disappointment and intolerance, illness and sadness, the whole gamut of motley abject emotions arise from *within* architecture, and typically in the act of habitation. After all, that 'monstrous excess' which Grosz reckons 'defies the functionalism, the minimalism, the drive to economy and simplicity', and 'overflows that thin membrane separating the inside from the outside', might be life (and death) itself. [6]

Indeed an earlier work by Morton bears this out. A closed wooden box form sits in the crook of the gallery wall and floor. It's got a couple of doors secured with a hefty padlock. Evidently, it's the opening to a downstairs room, a cellar. As one approaches, however, the box begins to rock, violently, the doors straining at the lock. Beastly sounds can be heard inside, and a ghoulish green light emanates from the cracks in the woodwork. This underground beast threatening to escape through the cracks and gaps is a fine figure of Grosz's

Elizabeth Grosz, 'Architectures of Excess', *Architecture from the Outside*, MIT Press, Massachusetts, 2001, p.153.

Quoted in Joseph A Barry, 'Report on the American Battle Between Good and Bad Modern Houses', *House Beautiful #95*, May 1953, p.270.

Edith Farnsworth, 'Memoirs', unpublished manuscript in three notebooks, Farnsworth Collection, Newberry Library, Chicago, ch.11, np. Excerpts published in Alice T. Friedman, 'People Who Live in Glass Houses', in *Women and the Making of the Modern House*, Abrams, New York, pp.128-159.

Beatriz Colomina, *Publicity and Privacy: Modern Architecture and Mass Media*, MIT Press, Massachusetts, 1996, p.9.

Grosz, op.cit., p.156.

Ibid, p.165 & 162.

Above: *Farnshaven, Illinois* 2001
From the series *Local +/or General*
Digital print
59.4 x 85 cm (image size)
Edition of 30
Image courtesy the artist and Roslyn Oxley9 Gallery,
Sydney; Anna Schwartz Gallery, Melbourne;
Gimpel Fils, London; Karyn Lovegrove Gallery,
Los Angeles

Right: *International Style Compound* 2000
Installation view, Museum of Contemporary Art,
Sydney
Image courtesy the artist and
Museum of Contemporary Art
Photo: Greg Weight

description. And indeed, much of Morton's early work uses architectural apertures to frame the escape of banal or quotidian or even 'monstrous' content. In *Now and Then* (1997), behind three sets of sliding glass doors set into a white plaster wall, one could faintly hear the extraneous sounds of pop music, a couple having sex, dogs barking. In *Accademia* (1998), a scale version of the suburban garage in St Kilda where Bon Scott, lead-singer with legendary rock band AC/DC from 1974 to 1980, used to live, one could hear the bands' repertoire being rehearsed by an exuberant fan.

In every case the real story quite literally exceeds the architectural form. To this

extent, Morton works with others – particularly architectural historians, but also novelists, theorists, filmmakers – who are part of a generation involved in critically revising the history of architecture, re-engaging the excessive detail, releasing the pent-up stories surrounding not only the design and production of buildings, but their public reception and habitation, including their frequent failure to deliver on Utopian aims and the perversion of ideal forms and ideas.

In 1965, Le Corbusier swam out to sea and drowned. He was staying at his 'holiday shack' at the time, Cabanon, built at Cap Martin overlooking the Mediterranean Sea; and overlooking the

property of fellow architect Eileen Gray and her partner Jean Badovici. They were once friends but Beatriz Colomina also suggests that Le Corbusier became fixated upon Gray, and she documents his 'occupation' of her by other than sexual means (since she was gay): the uncorrected attribution of Gray's building to Le Corbusier (even in Le Corbusier's own writings); the series of eight painted murals Le Corbusier executed across the walls of the building after Gray had left, which Gray regarded as vandalism of her design, and which featured portraits of Gray and Badovici with their impossible progeny; the misspelling of her name when ultimately Le Corbusier does concede to her; and finally the design and construction of his cabin on the verge of Gray's property, overlooking her house. [7]

Morton's model of Cabanon is perched atop a tall plinth overlooking all around. From inside we can hear a heartbeat. Peeking through the small window, through which Le Corbusier no doubt looked out upon Gray and Badovici, we can see an electrical bulb registering brain activity (more genius thoughts or indolent

sexual reverie). Whatever, the heart beats faster and faster until eventually it arrests – there's no brain function either – describing either sex or death, reflecting the final ambivalent scenario for Le Corbusier. In this scenario, Cabanon emerges as the locus of Le Corbusier's sexual perversion and creative drive, a twisted-love-shack on the top of the hill, where he sought inspiration looking out over the landscape and Gray, a 'maternal-feminine ground' no less.

If the basis of Western architecture lies with Vitruvius, in the conjunction of the human body and Euclidean geometry, it is then hardly surprising to find the repeated hetero-sexualisation of this paradigm within an institution that has been dominated by men. Such that when Vitruvius suggests that correct proportion derives from 'a man placed flat on his back with his hands and feet extended', we can understand the entire aesthetic of architecture as it derives from a prone, vulnerable body. [8]

In the case of Casa Malaparte, it's the body of Brigitte Bardot. *Oh Brigitte* refers

Beatriz Colomina, 'Battle Lines E.1027',
www.architecture.auckland.ac.nz/publications/inter-
stices/i4/THEHTML/keynotes/front.htm

Pollio Marcus Vitruvius, *The Ten Books on
Architecture*, trans. Morris Hicky Morgan, Harvard
University Press, Cambridge, 1914, p.73.

Top left: Garage, Dalgety Street, St Kilda, Melbourne
Image courtesy the artist
Photo: the artist

Above: Cabanon, Cap Martin
© Roberto Schezen/Esto
Photo: Roberto Schezen

Top right: *Cabanon and on and on...* 2002-03
Wood, Perspex, Milliput, resin, acrylic paint,
light, sound
47 x 50 x 40 cm
Collection of Zahava Elenberg &
Callum Fraser, Melbourne
Image courtesy the artist and
Anna Schwartz Gallery, Melbourne
Photo: Richard Crompton

Right: *Cabanon and on and on...* 2002-03
(interior detail)
Image courtesy the artist and
Anna Schwartz Gallery, Melbourne
Photo: Richard Crompton

directly to Jean-Luc Godard's film, *Contempt*, which casts Bardot – at her peak in 1963 – against the structure of Casa Malaparte, and the natural beauty of Capri beyond. Indeed, the house, which hugs a jutting rock promontory, is repeatedly compared to Bardot's body, splayed along beds and lounges inside. The two contoured landscapes combine (just like the view from Cabanon). Yet rather than inspire the husband-scriptwriter (Michel Piccoli), who has stalled in his attempts to complete a rewrite of Homer's *Odyssey* for an American movie mogul (Jack Palance), the remote and beautiful surrounds prolong his ordeal, stifle his creativity and turn his wife's love into contempt.

The film refers in part to Curzio Malaparte's life as an ambivalent dilettante who worked across media throughout the world as a novelist, journalist, filmmaker, and as the architect of the Casa (along with Libera, who was involved in sketching first versions of the house). Malaparte's shifting allegiances are also renowned; a Fascist sympathiser during the war (which arguably gained him the extraordinary site), he later became a Maoist, donating the House to the People's Republic of China, before finally converting to Catholicism on his death-bed in 1957.

Morton's model sits on an enormous rock jutting out of the gallery wall,

confirming the diminutive scale of the house, which is ostensibly a 'rational' box form that sits bravely but hopelessly within the awesome and overwhelming terrain. And what could compare to the surrounding beauty – a novel, a film, a painting, radical politics? Like the building, none of these poetic forms could contain the sublime experience, and the inspiration sought by many at the Casa could also be an unbearable, unendurable intensity, comparable to a prison. Indeed, Malaparte lived there only sporadically. He wrote in his novel *The Skin* in 1949, comparing it to his imprisonment in the war: 'I now live on an island in a melancholy, austere house, which I have built myself on a solitary cliff by the sea. The image of my longing.' Thus the Casa is not an architecture of abundant fulfillment for the occupant, as its wonderful location might suggest, but an architecture of constant yearning for the elusive muse. Like Cabanon, the model is animated by the rise and fall of sexual desire in an endless cycle. And so to the erotic murmur of the work's title, the model answers 'Silenzio!', as does the film, this final word uttered while the

camera pans across the roof and comes to rest on the horizon.

Morton's architecture speaks volumes. The Gas and Fuel Corporation Towers in Melbourne once formed the southern perimeter of the CBD, their twin faces rising from the ground like enormous screens, their rectilinear, gridded repetition an anthem for city workers and the industry beyond. Too blunt and too brutal for many, the hard-core modernist towers were razed to the ground, making way for recent developments including Federation Square, a new plaza-style civic space and a good example of what one architect friend called 'postmodern architecture eating itself'. Morton's model of the original buildings, *Gas and Fuel* 2002, revives memories of the city before its grand transformation by state politicians with a billion dollars. Indeed, the model is animated by a small child's voice crying out within 'Help Me! Help Me! Please Help Me!'. It's unclear whether the voice issues from a lost child within, or is the voice of the building – or of the epoch – crying out for attention in the wake of

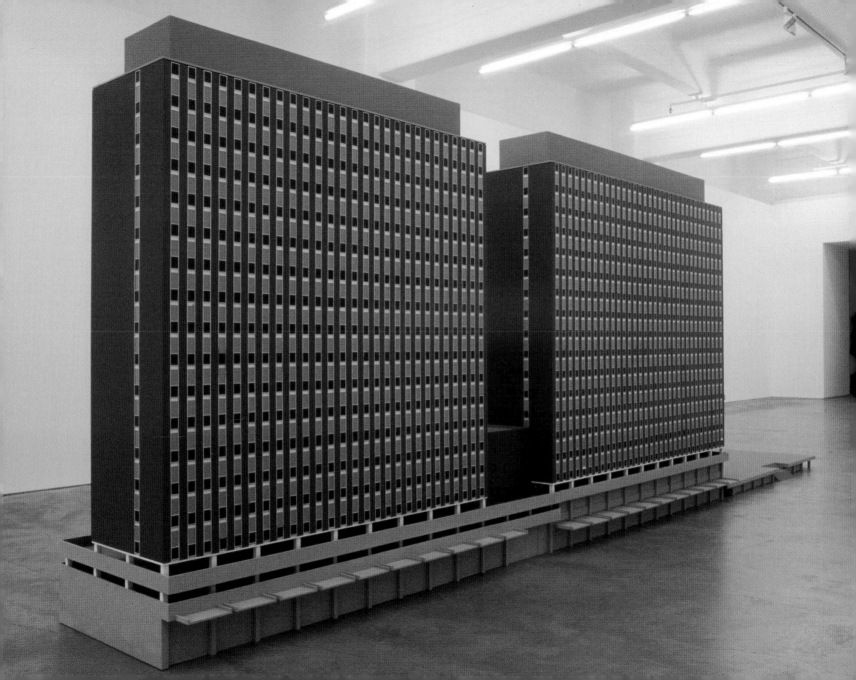

Left: *Gas and Fuel* 2002
Wood, acrylic, aluminium,
synthetic polymer paint, light, sound
220 x 91 x 600 cm
Corbett Lyon and Yueji Lyon Collection
Image courtesy the artist and Anna Schwartz Gallery,
Melbourne
Photo: Robert Colvin

Right: *Cottage Industry: Bawdy Nights* 1999
Wood, Perspex, Milliput, acrylic paint, light, sound
55 x 80 x 30 cm
Private collection
Image courtesy the artist and
Anna Schwartz Gallery, Melbourne
Photo: Kenneth Pleban

modernism's devolution and practical neglect. In either case, Morton's work is a ghostly figment of a period past, but which persists in its trace effects.

For example, the work was purchased by the original architect's nephew and bequeathed to the new National Gallery of Victoria Australia, built on Federation Square where the original buildings once stood. The irony of the diminutive voice also becomes clearer. In fact, it's a line taken from the 1986 movie *The Fly*: Jeff Goldblum's last hopeless cry for help following his transmogrification from human to man/fly hybrid. But its resemblance to a child's voice, perhaps a lost child within, is also keyed to its

new location since one of the most popular images in the State Collection, occasionally exhibited in these new premises, is Frederick McCubbin's 1886 painting *Lost*, a young girl in a blue bonnet, alone in the bush. It's part of a long tradition in which hapless juvenile colonials disappear in the antipodes, celebrated in films like *Walkabout* or novels such as *Picnic at Hanging Rock*.

We can also hear kids in Morton's version of the United Nations headquarters in New York. The original building by Wallace K Harrison typifies a pragmatic American incarnation of international style in an ultra-straight stacked 39-floor tower of green glass, book-ended with sheer

blank marble walls. The building provides office accommodation to 3,400 UN employees from around the world; a simple, massive form that offsets the flutter of national flags in front. The sound of children 'playing war' within returns the UN charter to its origins in the sandpit and the subsequent complexity of world politics is recast in terms of infantile rivalry, which could be either a virtue or a criticism. Whichever, in the simple substitution of content, architecture frames a mutable space within; precisely, an absence to be filled with endless, interchangeable routines. Just like a picture frame, it imparts especial significance to the often undeserving real events inside.

Apparently, there's an empty block where Captain James Cook, the first Englishman to arrive at Botany Bay in 1788, once lived as a child in Great Ayton in Yorkshire. The original house was dismantled stone by stone and shipped to Australia (indeed every brick was numbered) and then rebuilt in 1934, in Fitzroy Gardens, to commemorate the centenary of the founding of Melbourne whereupon it has become one of the most popular tourist attractions in Melbourne, even though it has negligible actual significance to the place. What now commends the building, apart from it being simply old, and the folly of relocating it, is the whole question of one culture imposing itself – including its

Top left: Gas and Fuel Building viewed from Batman Avenue, Melbourne 1996
© Image courtesy Ian H. Hill
Photo: Ian H. Hill

Above left to right:
United Nations Headquarters
© Lawrence A. Martin / GreatBuildings.com
Photo: Lawrence A. Martin

The numbering of the stones
Reproduced with the permission of Cook's Cottage management for the City of Melbourne
From *Cook's Cottage*, Alison Forbes, Melbourne, 1978, p.31.

Cook's Cottage, Melbourne
Courtesy the artist
Photo: The artist

Right: *Untitled* 2003
(with Nick Hubicki)
Installation view, Museum of Contemporary Art, Sydney
Wood, steel, acrylic, vinyl, synthetic polymer paint, sound
300 x 70 x 20 cm
Image courtesy the artist and Museum of Contemporary Art
Photo: Greg Weight

buildings – on some other ground, taking no account of the site. For which reason, I guess, Morton made a scale model of the cottage and returned it to the UK for an exhibition called The Queen is Dead.[9]

Morton's cottage alludes to a very different story however. The narrative within blends Cook's gentlemanly endeavours with the ribald antics of comedian Benny Hill in a sketch about the early history of settlement (think 'rum, sodomy and the lash'). Thus we hear Cook groan with sexual pleasure as he takes a whip to a couple of lassies and there ensues about eight minutes of orgiastic slapstick (which may well be the real gift of England to 'Australian' culture).

Morton's work is no model for the future as architectural models often are, but rather a model of the past as it accrues to the present. The future may occasionally be glimpsed, particularly in the digital print series Local+/or General, which combines various famous houses with multinational business franchises such that the Rose Seidler House is a McDonald's, the Rietveld House

⁹ Stills Gallery, Edinburgh, 1999
¹⁰ Alice T Friedman, op.cit., p.152.

becomes a Toys "R" Us, and the Farnsworth house is a 7-Eleven. These prints project the expansion of commerce into every singular, remarkable place on earth, these iconic homes notwithstanding. But while the combination might seem initially odd, there has never really been a clash between high and low, just the matter of their slow, constant mediation. Such as when in the 1960s Mobil employed Bauhaus graduate Eliot Noyes to design its service stations. So too, Morton's prints and models expand the applications of modernist design to all sorts of global enterprise almost exactly as it was intended.

It's not surprising then to find a gas station based on Philip Johnson's Glass House from 1949. In Morton's model, Gas 2003, that classic building's original articulated form comprising the main and guest houses, and pool, linked by various scenic routes, is now a drive-in store with a canopy extending over fuel pumps, an adjacent garage workshop, and a twinkling pool of petrol that collects from a leaking bowser-hose

lying on the asphalt surface. The purity of form and ideas at work in Johnson's 'gay domestic campus'[10] – an open and transparent building for daytime, a totally closed building for the evenings – seems debased by the vulgar necessity of automobile societies and roadside retail. However Morton's model simply elaborates the implicit Fordism of Johnson's own multi-functional design at New Canaan, which separated component buildings according to lifestyle requirements.

It's the perfect awkward setting for an unspecified drama; the stage for tremendous explosive violence, figured subtly in the dangerous, pooling petrol. Somewhere inside a radio is playing; sweet, saccharine muzak over and over. It's a still, suspended moment; interminable. It's as if we are waiting for a bomb to go off, watching natural resources dwindle in a diminishing, desolate landscape, an environmental disaster looming, not knowing that calamity is just seconds away, ignorant of what has gone just before we arrive on the scene. Thus the total

reverberant, poetic effect of Gas is a generalised anxiety at the prevailing uncertainty of modern life, extrapolated from the inversion of aesthetic values at its core, that is, the volatile mix of high and low motifs. It's an image of the world's various traumas trickling down in a small, off-centre, elegiac moment.

Typically, architectural models suppress the grim realities of life. The gardens are neat, the people are healthy and well off, and the weather is nice. This is consistent with the idealism of architects, generally, in providing buildings that will improve our lives. However the attributes of life within Morton's models are in stark contrast: bondage and deviance, murder,

monsters, arguments, bad TV and movies, lost and helpless children, junk food, low end consumption, death. Truly, it's a litany of monstrous, bestial excess. And yet these elements do ultimately combine to some positive effect.

Habitat is a 1:50 architectural scale model of a mass housing project of the same name that was built in 1967 for Expo in Montreal, Canada, by the Israeli architect Moshe Safdie. Habitat consisted of 354 modular construction units making up 158 houses, containing, in all, 16 different housing types.

Habitat today is an exclusive 'designer' apartment complex. But it was first

Above: Moshe Safdie
Habitat '67
Montreal, Canada
John Bland Canadian Architecture Collection
McGill University, Montreal
© Moshe Safdie and Associates
Photo: Timothy Hursley

proposed as a Utopian housing project, suffused with the communitarian ethics of the late '60s. It developed out of Safdie's 1961 MA thesis at McGill University, and his interest in the radical redesign of the urban environment in line with the complexity of lived reality. In Habitat, the unitary structures could be varied systematically to account for different people's lives, and mass housing was therefore individualised to accommodate a range of lifestyles and user types, with larger 'family' apartments set alongside single units.

Morton's model comprises 310 different mass-produced units, affixed according to Safdie's original plans, to represent 116 of the apartments. Some of these contain lights and sounds, programmed to suggest an imaginary day in the life of the complex, and a day in the lives of the many people who might live in such a building. For example, as the sun rises, waves of life break across the façade. We hear alarm clocks, morning ablutions, telephones ringing. We see lights coming on, conversations ensuing, people laughing, people yelling.

Pages 21–23: *Habitat* 2003
Installation views, National Gallery of
Victoria Australia, Melbourne
Wood, aluminium, acrylic paint, light, sound
74 x 660 x 130 cm
Courtesy of the Corbett Lyon and
Yueji Lyon Collection
Images courtesy the artist and
National Gallery of Victoria
Photos: Helen Oliver-Skuse

Some fights break out. People leave for work. The day wears on. Someone plays loud music. People shout, dogs bark, babies cry. As evening grows, people come home, lights dim and television sets begin to flicker. Finally, reparations are made, and calm returns to the building. So a day passes in a cycle of about 28 minutes (that is, 1/50th day). But this same 'Groundhog Day' passes repeatedly, infinitely.

The denizens of Morton's model are locked within this diminutive scale and accelerated time frame, bound to do the same things day-in, day-out, caught in a cycle of unending domestic conflict, set against a distant dream of community living. They are characters unable to reach escape velocity from the orbital pull of their daily routine and entrenched cynicism, despite the best intentions of architects. However, as the drama unfolds, resolves and repeats, we also sense new dreams arising from the disagreements, a profound relenting to life's true grit. And Morton finds this small, indefatigable hope between the architect's schemata

for social transformation and the plebeian routines of the species; precisely, in-between the dream of architecture and the reality of life on earth. He figures the shape or form of this hope as a double-helix, or Moebius strip, as it springs eternal but is bound to fail, looping back to where it starts, the reason we go on day after day, not so much a form of progress as a tempo or pulse keyed to celestial movements.

And so in the model, the cycle of light and sound, day and night, the concert of lives, the refrain of sorrow, anger, grief and exhaustion, is reiterated across the honeycomb facade like a grand symphonic chorale, which rises and falls according to some perpetual, inbuilt species' rhythm. And in this whorl of living the building comes alive, like a hive. Which is the whole story and the fate of any building. Eventually it disappears in the flurry of activity, inside, outside, and around it; outside architecture, indeed, well beyond it.

Stuart Koop
Curator

Above: *Down the Hatch* 2003
Installation views, Hamburger Bahnhof, Berlin
Polystyrene, expanding foam, epoxy,
steel enamel paint
Dimensions variable
Images courtesy the artist and
Hamburger Bahnhof
Photos: Jens Ziehe

Right: *Toys "R" Us, Utrecht* 2001
From the series *Local +/or General*
Digital print
59.4 x 85 cm (image size)
Edition of 30
Image courtesy the artist and Roslyn Oxley9 Gallery,
Sydney; Anna Schwartz Gallery, Melbourne;
Gimpel Fils, London; Karyn Lovegrove Gallery,
Los Angeles

Above: *Cul-de-sac* 1994
Wood, brick panels, plasterboard, acrylic paint, light
Dimensions variable
Image courtesy the artist
Photo: Richard Crompton

Right: *Accademia* 1998
Wood, plasterboard, glass, steel,
render, enamel, plastic, sound
405 x 418 x 127 cm
Image courtesy the artist
Photo: Andrius Lipsyus

Above: *Belvedere* 1995
Installation view, Art Gallery of NSW, Sydney
Wood, cement, glass, steel, synthetic polymer paint
600 x 150 x 70 cm
Image courtesy the artist
Photo: Christopher Snee

Right: *Best Western* 2003
From the series *Interbau Wow Wow*
Digital print
94.5 x 170 cm (image size)
Edition of 30
Image courtesy the artist and Roslyn Oxley9 Gallery,
Sydney; Anna Schwartz Gallery, Melbourne;
Gimpel Fils, London; Karyn Lovegrove Gallery,
Los Angeles

Above: *Billyput* 2003
Installation view, Govett Brewster Art Gallery, New
Plymouth, New Zealand
Wood, steel, synthetic polymer paint, sound
104 x 44 cm
Image courtesy the artist and
Govett Brewster Art Gallery
Photo: Bryan James

Right: *The Heights* 1995
Wood, steel, glass, render, enamel
200 x 875 x 70 cm
Image courtesy the artist and Karyn Lovegrove
Gallery, Los Angeles
Photo: Mark Ashkanazy

Above: *24 hrs* 1995
Wood, steel, canvas, rope, synthetic
polymer paint and enamel on wood
175 x 220 x 70 cm
Collection Monash University Museum of Art,
Melbourne
Image courtesy the artist and Karyn Lovegrove
Gallery, Los Angeles
Photo: Andrew Curtis

Right: *Mac Attack, Wahroonga, NSW* 2001
From the series *Local +/or General*
Digital print
59.4 x 85 cm (image size)
Edition of 30
Image courtesy the artist and Roslyn Oxley9 Gallery,
Sydney; Anna Schwartz Gallery, Melbourne;
Gimpel Fils, London; Karyn Lovegrove Gallery,
Los Angeles

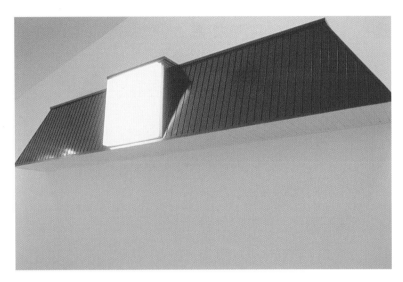

Above: *Convenience* 1996
Wood, lightbox, enamel
80 x 480 x 50 cm
Image courtesy the artist and
Roslyn Oxley9 Gallery, Sydney
Photo: John Brash

Right: *Lockout* 1998
Installation view, CBD Gallery, Sydney
Vinyl, cardboard
Dimensions variable
Image courtesy the artist
Photo: the artist

Above: *Cottage Industry: Bawdy Nights* 1999 (detail)
Image courtesy the artist and
Anna Schwartz Gallery, Melbourne
Photo: Kenneth Pleban

Right: *Glenville Souvenirs, Mt Irvine, NSW* 2001
From the series *Local +/or General*
Digital print
59.4 x 85 cm (image size)
Edition of 30
Image courtesy the artist and Roslyn Oxley9 Gallery,
Sydney; Anna Schwartz Gallery, Melbourne;
Gimpel Fils, London; Karyn Lovegrove Gallery,
Los Angeles

Estrada Das Liberdade, Rio de Janeiro 2001
From the series *Local +/or General*
Digital print
54 x 150 cm (image size)
Edition of 30
Image courtesy the artist and Roslyn Oxley9 Gallery,
Sydney; Anna Schwartz Gallery, Melbourne;
Gimpel Fils, London; Karyn Lovegrove Gallery,
Los Angeles

International Style 1999
1:4 scale version
Installation view, Santa Monica Museum of Art,
Los Angeles
Wood, acrylic, synthetic polymer paint, light, sound
130 x 780 x 440 cm
Image courtesy the artist and Karyn Lovegrove
Gallery, Los Angeles
Photo: Joshua White

Above: *Next to Nothing* 2000
Wood, mirrored perspex, acrylic, lights, sound
163 x 154 x 122 cm
Collection Gimpel Fils, London
Image courtesy the artist and
Roslyn Oxley9 Gallery, Sydney
Photo: Richard Crompton

Right: *Continental Girls, Paris* 2001
From the series *Local +/or General*
Digital print
59.4 x 85 cm (image size)
Edition of 30
Image courtesy the artist and Roslyn Oxley9 Gallery,
Sydney; Anna Schwartz Gallery, Melbourne;
Gimpel Fils, London; Karyn Lovegrove Gallery,
Los Angeles

Above:
Bellvue 1998
Wood, acrylic, curtains
200 x 875 x 50 cm
Private collection
Image courtesy the artist
Photo: Haru Sameshima

Right: *Motormouth* 2002
Installation views, Art Gallery of NSW, Sydney
Polystyrene, high impact polyurethane,
plastic, resin, oil stick, sound
Dimensions variable
Collection Art Gallery of NSW
Image courtesy the artist and
Roslyn Oxley9 Gallery Sydney
Photograph: Diana Panuccio

Above: *Oh Brigitte* 2002
Image courtesy the artist and
Anna Schwartz Gallery, Melbourne
Photo: Robert Colvin

Right: *Casa Spizzico, Capri* 2001
From the series *Local +/or General*
Digital print
59.4 x 85 cm (image size)
Edition of 30
Image courtesy the artist and Roslyn Oxley9 Gallery,
Sydney; Anna Schwartz Gallery, Melbourne;
Gimpel Fils, London; Karyn Lovegrove Gallery,
Los Angeles

Above: *Gas and Fuel* 2002
Image courtesy the artist and
Anna Schwartz Gallery, Melbourne
Photo: Robert Colvin

Right: *Tropicana* 2003
From the series *Interbau Wow Wow*
Digital print
94.5 x 170 cm (image size)
Edition of 30
Image courtesy the artist and Roslyn Oxley9 Gallery,
Sydney; Anna Schwartz Gallery, Melbourne;
Gimpel Fils, London; Karyn Lovegrove Gallery,
Los Angeles

Above: *Gas* 2003
Installation view, Museum of Contemporary Art,
Sydney
Image courtesy the artist and
Museum of Contemporary Art
Photo: Greg Weight

Right: *New Canaan, Connecticut* 2003
From the series *Local +/or General*
Digital print
75.5 x 150 cm
Edition of 30
Image courtesy the artist and Roslyn Oxley9 Gallery,
Sydney; Anna Schwartz Gallery, Melbourne;
Gimpel Fils, London; Karyn Lovegrove Gallery,
Los Angeles

Above: *Cabanon and on and on…* 2002-03
Image courtesy the artist and
Anna Schwartz Gallery, Melbourne
Photo: Richard Crompton

Right: *Cellar* 1998
Wood, acrylic, synthetic polymer paint,
motor, light, sound
40 x 80 x 150 cm
Image courtesy the artist and
Roslyn Oxley9 Gallery, Sydney
Photo: John Brash

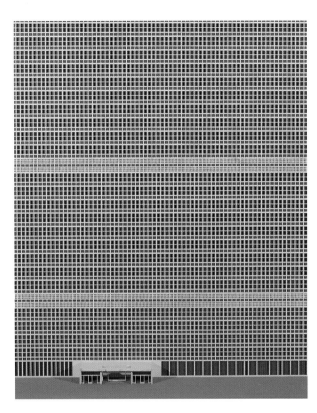

Above: *Untitled* 2003 (detail)
Installation view, Museum of Contemporary Art,
Sydney
Image courtesy the artist and
Museum of Contemporary Art
Photo: Greg Weight

Right: *Holiday Inn* 2003
From the series *Interbau Wow Wow*
Digital print
94.5 x 170 cm (image size)
Edition of 30
Image courtesy the artist and Roslyn Oxley9 Gallery,
Sydney; Anna Schwartz Gallery, Melbourne;
Gimpel Fils, London; Karyn Lovegrove Gallery,
Los Angeles

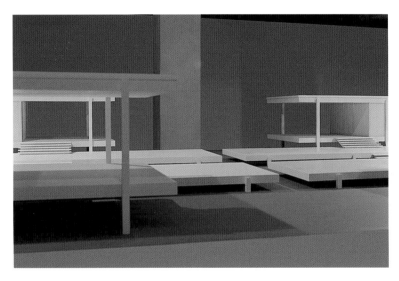

Above: *International Style Compound* 2000-01
Installation view, Museum of Contemporary Art,
Sydney
Image courtesy the artist and
Museum of Contemporary Art
Photo: Greg Weight

Right: *Eames Depot, Nevada* 2001
From the series *Local +/or General*
Digital print
59.4 x 85 cm (image size)
Edition of 30
Image courtesy the artist and Roslyn Oxley9 Gallery,
Sydney; Anna Schwartz Gallery, Melbourne;
Gimpel Fils, London; Karyn Lovegrove Gallery,
Los Angeles

Pages 58–59: *Habitat* 2003
Installation view, National Gallery of Victoria
Australia, Melbourne
Image courtesy the artist and
National Gallery of Victoria
Photo: Helen Oliver-Skuse

THE CITY IS A SEWER

Playing on a television somewhere in the world is a documentary on architecture. There's probably a British voice-narration. It's probably funded by European cable companies. The Americans will buy it cheap. This British guy will undoubtedly be anthropological about architecture. He'll use some standard line about how Man lived in caves, covering its walls with his own excrement. A wry tone in his voice will marvel at how far we have progressed.

But we still live in caves. We've just renamed them homes. Some even pay architects to design their homes for them. If living in caves is making walls out of your excreta, then getting an architect to design your home is having your bum wiped for you.

Living with human waste is a basic *modus* of the *domus*. Behind every living abode is a place where that waste has to be organised: the toilet. For most, this involves a disappearing act. It's pure magic: you'll never have to clean up your own excreta, but you can still live with it. Your walls aren't made of the stuff any more, but they are signs of the invisibility of it. The most stringent council regulations are those connected to waste disposal. Your house extends its colon into the bowels of the earth and to sewerage farms far away from your domain.

Just as your discharge is jettisoned laterally away from you in the private sphere, your collective excrescence is linearly projected about you in the public sphere. Public architecture – the glowing orb of Man's sophisticated endeavour – throws itself up around you at every move in the city. Like the smell at the sewerage farm, it clouds the air. In the city centre, it blocks the sun, casts ominous shadows, and impedes all traversing. These buildings are the visibility of that which your home hides.

Such gilded gargantuans of verticality have long been associated with the phallic. Even our repressed British voice-over narrator will make such a quip. Men, women and children all marvel and mock the phallic these days, as if there is profound insight in a lazy

Freudian association of an erect cock with something that stands erect. (Besides which, if buildings were actively phallic, they would be sticking out horizontally.) In the collective mind of the architectural guild, maybe architects' cocks are 30 stories high. The reality is more likely to be millimetres.

Big buildings are neither phallic nor penile – residues of a failed attempt to ascribe symbolic weight to their form. Read as morphological signage, they are best viewed as human excrement that has been piled up. High. This gravity-defying feat is a testament not to Man's ingenuity, inventiveness or inspiration, but to the excessive amount of bowel movement he can induce. The public landscape is the sewerage farm you've heard so much about but never visited. The spread of tall buildings are not monuments to architects but extruded columnar charts indicating the growth of the city: the more people, the more shit, the taller the buildings. The excreta that once covered the cave walls is now ritualised into an effluvia that binds the heavens to earth in the monumental skyline of the stinking city.

Artists can be rightly accused of playing with their own stools and sludge. Grand narratives might link Prometheus to the sculptor and his clay, but the child who marvels at his own waste is a closer model for idle artistic endeavour. As architects make greater claims for their artistic discourse, and artists morph installation practice into virtual architecture, a splatter-ball battle ensues, each hurling the other's discharge back at the other. Space becomes inverted, as architects design galleries that look like magnified *objet d'art* from the outside, while artists toil away inside setting up art that resembles demolition zones, construction sites and renovation schemes. Far from being a phenomenon of postmodern fusion and integration, this battle for the city within and without the museum is mostly a neurotic territorial collision. It's a spectator sport worthy of any televisual enterprise – but flicking the channel might be the best option.

Callum Morton's work plays on a different channel. Joining the regurgitative impulse of the artist, the

time-consuming syndrome of the artisan, and the heroic expulsion of the architect, Morton places small but potent turds downwind in the museum. They accrue the stench of the city's prize-winning architectural edifices, intensifying their odour through essencing their form in his maximalized miniatures and transmogrified turrets. Feeling the air currents cartographically formed by the city's wind tunnels, Morton's schematics, models and installations strategically pinpoint the intersections where architectural voiding has left its mark – and where the city reveals itself as sewer.

Philip Brophy
Philip Brophy is a filmmaker, composer and writer based in Melbourne.

LIST OF WORKS

Untitled 2003
(with Nick Hubicki)
Wood, steel, acrylic, vinyl,
synthetic polymer paint, sound
300 x 70 x 20 cm
Courtesy of the artist and
Roslyn Oxley9 Gallery, Sydney

Gas 2003
Wood, steel, Perspex, resin, acrylic
paint, light, sound
55 x 418 x 474 cm
Muzak composed by Philip Brophy
Courtesy of the artist and
Anna Schwartz Gallery, Melbourne

Habitat 2003
Wood, aluminium, acrylic paint,
light, sound
74 x 660 x 130 cm
Courtesy of the Corbett Lyon and
Yueji Lyon Collection

Cabanon and on and on... 2002-03
Wood, Perspex, Milliput, resin,
acrylic paint, light, sound
47 x 50 x 40 cm
Collection of Zahava Elenberg &
Callum Fraser, Melbourne

Oh Brigitte 2001
Wood, Perspex, polystyrene, high
impact poly-urethane coating, metal,
plastic, acrylic paint, light, sound
120 x 150 x 90 cm
Collection of Anna & Morry Schwartz,
Melbourne

International Style Compound 2000–01
Wood, aluminium, Perspex, paper,
acrylic paint, light, sound
52 x 654 x 382 cm
Courtesy of the Corbett Lyon and Yueji
Lyon Collection

Cottage Industry: Bawdy Nights 1999
Wood, Perspex, epoxy, acrylic paint,
light, sound
55 x 80 x 30 cm
Private Collection. Courtesy Anna
Schwartz Gallery, Melbourne

CALLUM MORTON

Selected Group Exhibitions

2003 *Face Up*, Hamburger Bahnhof, Berlin, Germany; *Come In*, Govett-Brewster Art Gallery, New Plymouth, New Zealand; *Architectural Allusions* (Callum Morton and Edwin Zwakman), Gimpel Fils, London, UK; *Twilight*, Gimpel Fils, London, UK; *salon des refuses. Progetti di public art mai realizzati*, Fondazione Bevilacqua La Masa, Venice, Italy

2002 *Fieldwork: Australian Art 1968–2002*, National Gallery of Victoria Australia, Melbourne; *The Heimlich Unheimlich*, RMIT University Gallery, Melbourne; *People Places and Ideas*, Monash University Museum of Art, Melbourne; *Bittersweet*, Art Gallery of New South Wales, Sydney; *Nocturne*, Mornington Regional Art Gallery, Victoria; *Gulliver's Travels*, CAST Gallery, Hobart, and touring nationally

2001 *Feature*, Govett-Brewster Art Gallery, New Plymouth, New Zealand; *The (Ideal) Home Show*, Gimpel Fils, London, UK

2000 *Longevity*, Ian Potter Museum of Art, Melbourne; *The Retrieved Object*, Linden Gallery, Melbourne; *Rent*, Overgaden, Copenhagen, Denmark/Australian Centre for Contemporary Art, Melbourne; *August 26*, Elastic, Sydney

1999 *Signs of Life*, Melbourne International Biennial, Melbourne; *Facsimile*, LAC Gallery, Caracas, Venezuela; *The Queen is Dead*, Stills Gallery, Edinburgh, UK; *The Persistence of Pop*, Monash University Gallery, Melbourne

1998 *Everybody Knows*, Openspace and Care of Spazio d'arte contemporanea, Milan, Italy; *Strolling: the art of arcades, boulevards, barricades, publicity*, Museum of Modern Art at Heide, Melbourne; *Every Other Day*, Roslyn Oxley9 Gallery, Sydney; *Snapshot*, 1st Floor, Melbourne; *Proscenium*, Artspace, Auckland, New Zealand; *Rough Trade*, Plimsoll Gallery, Hobart

1997 *Seppelt Contemporary Art Award*, Museum of Contemporary Art, Sydney; *Power Corruption and Lies*, Institute of Modern Art, Brisbane; *World Speak Dumb*, Karyn Lovegrove Gallery, Melbourne; *Art <=> Advertising*, Robert Lindsay Gallery, Melbourne

1996 *Power Corruption and Lies / New Order Factory Records 1981*, Plötz Gallery, Brisbane; *The Expanded Field* (with Danius Kesminas and Anna Nervegna), 200 Gertrude St, Melbourne; *Ruins in Reverse*, RMIT Gallery, Melbourne

1995 *Perspectives: 200 Gertrude Street 1985-1995*, 200 Gertrude Street, Melbourne; *The Object of Existence*, Australian Centre for Contemporary Art, Melbourne; *Lyndal Walker and Callum Morton*, 1st Floor, Melbourne; *Australian Perspecta*, Art Gallery of New South Wales, Sydney; *Videonnale #6*, Bonn, Germany

1994 *Projection: Filming the Body*, The Basement Project, Melbourne; *Passage: Spatial Interventions*, Monash University Gallery, Melbourne; *Loop: Part One*: A Critical Cities Project, Longford Cinema, Melbourne; *The Exact Moment*, A Critical Cities Project, Melbourne

1991 *#100*, Store 5, Melbourne; *Magasin 5*, Cannibal Pierce Galerie Australienne, Paris, France; *March On!* (#2) (with Rose Nolan), Store 5, Melbourne

1989/ 1990 *#62, #31,#11*, Store 5, Melbourne

Selected Bibliography

2003 Edward Colless, 'Callum Morton: Interior World', *Australian Art Collector* no. 25, Sydney, pp 46-49

Stuart Koop, 'Groundhog Day', *Habitat*, exhibition catalogue, National Gallery of Victoria Australia, Melbourne

Andrew Mackenzie, 'Messing with Mies', *Broadsheet* no. 34, Adelaide, pp 24-25

Daniel Palmer, 'Callum Morton', *Frieze* no. 72, London, p.106

2002 Nick Hubicki, 'Conning Icons', *Architectural Review Australia*, Spring, pp. 20-21

2001 Stuart Koop, 'International Style', *Monument* no. 41, Sydney, pp. 94-97

1999 *Mixed Business: The Work of Callum Morton*, exhibition catalogue, Santa Monica Museum of Art, Los Angeles

Karen Burns, 'Urban Unease: The Work of Callum Morton' (unpublished), Melbourne

Max Delany, 'Raising the Dead: An Interview with Callum Morton', *Like Art Magazine* no. 10, Melbourne, pp.20-25

Juliana Engberg (ed.), *Signs of Life*, Melbourne International Biennial, exhibition catalogue, Melbourne

1997 Giovanni Intra, *now and then*, exhibition catalogue, Govett-Brewster Art Gallery, New Plymouth, New Zealand

Stuart Koop, 'Three Quarter Time: Interview with Callum Morton', *Seppelt Contemporary Art Award*, exhibition catalogue, Museum of Contemporary Art, Sydney

1995 Max Delany, 'Callum Morton: Belvedere', *Australian Perspecta 95* exhibition catalogue, Art Gallery of New South Wales, Sydney

Stuart Koop, 'Real Model World', *Art & Text* no. 52, Sydney, p. 36-38

MCA Ambassadors

The MCA gratefully acknowledges the generosity of Ambassadors, whose annual donations support the solo exhibitions of emerging and established artists in the level 4 galleries, the associated catalogues and educations programs.

Visionaries
American Express
Telstra
Geoff & Vicki Ainsworth
David & Michelle Coe
Loti & Victor Smorgon
Anonymous

Innovators
Ginny & Leslie Green
Dr Edward & Mrs Cynthia Jackson
Matthew Howison
Malcolm & Lucy Turnbull

Futurists
Neil & Diane Balnaves
Dr Colin & Mrs Liz Laverty
Ann Lewis AM
Reg & Sally Richardson
Anonymous

Contemporaries
Antoinette Albert
Michele Asprey & Lindsay Powers
Mr & Mrs Daniel Besen
Dr Bruce Caldwell
Andrew & Cathy Cameron
Susan Cato
Leo Christie & Marion Borgelt
Patrick Corrigan AM
Jane Dawson
Daniel & Lyndell Droga
Michele Ferguson & Michael Magnus
Sandra & Paul Ferman
Nina Field

If you would like to find out more about the Ambassadors program please call the MCA on +61 (0)2 9250 8414.

Leon Fink & Jenny Turpin
Simon Goh
Stephen Grant & Bridget Pirrie
Tony Green
Linda Gregoriou
Catherine Harris
Angelo & Despina Hatsatouris
Michael Hawker
Jean Herron
Cherry Hood & Graham Jones
Art Equity
Andrew Horsley
Maunsell Hughes Gallery
Dr John & Mrs Mary Indyk
Davina Jackson & Chris Johnson
Judy Joye
Erika Jumikis
Christina Kennedy
Michael King
Isabella Klompé
Doug & Sue Knox
Christopher Kuan
Ujin Lee
Harvey Light
Andrew & Amanda Love
Richard Ludbrook
Jenny Manton
Nicky & Bruce McWilliam
Suzanne & Warwick Miller
Jennifer & Stephen Mills
Daniel Moquay & Prof Rotraut Klein
The Annabel & Ruper Myer Foundation
Lisa Paulsen
Andrew & Chloe Podgornik
Dr Dick Quan
Crispin Rice
Susan Rothwell
Penelope Seidler
Ian Hill & Morna Seres
Vivienne Sharpe
Dr Gene & Mr Brian Sherman

Gillian Simon & Darren Kindrachuk
Paul & Dalia Sinclair
Ezekiel Solomon
Paul Sumner
Robyn Thurston
Isaac & Susan Wakil
Josie & John Walton AM
Michael Whitworth & Candice Bruce
Neil & Jill Wilson
Gregory Woolley
Anonymous

Initiators
Gordon Darling AO CMG & Marilyn Darling
Helen Eager
Michael & Doris Hobbs
Stephanie Houstein
Gary Langsford
David Maloney & Erin Flaherty
Anthony & Suzanne Maple-Brown
Tetsuji Narita
Peter & Maree Thomas
Dr Gerard Wain & Dr Veronique Lajoie
Lex Watson

Supporters
Dr Jennifer Arnold
Baz & Keltie Archer
Greg & Angela Baster
Bobbe Bowman Zeleny
Natalia Bradshaw
Tanya & Mark Carnegie
Emily Carney
Sophie Dalgleish
Peter Fay
Penny Field
Annette Freeman
Dr Mark Gianoutsos
Chris Goffin
Leo & Paula Gothelf
Sophia Guest
Robert & Lori Harrison

Ashley Hempsall
Mark Isaacs
Victor Kay
Douglas Kippax
Paul Kornmehl
Anne Kwasner
Paula Latos-Valier & Biron Valier
Gregory Lindsay-Owen
Annie Parnell
Clarissa Patterson
Liz Ragland
Lara Stella
Sarah Still
The Hon Peter Underhill OBE & Prof Nancy Underhill
Cassandra Wilkinson
Merrill & Scott Witt
Wye Yap
Katie Yuill

As at 13 August 2003

First published on the occasion of the exhibition
Callum Morton: More Talk about Buildings and Mood

Museum of Contemporary Art, Sydney
29 October 2003 – 26 January 2004

National Library of Australia Cataloguing-in-Publication data

Callum Morton : more talk about buildings and mood.

Bibliography.

ISBN 1 875632 89 1.

1. Morton, Callum, 1965- - Exhibitions. 2. Art, Modern - 20th century - Australia - Exhibitions.

I. Museum of Contemporary Art (Sydney, N.S.W.).

709.05

Guest Curator: Stuart Koop
Project Management: Russell Storer
Catalogue design: Miles Goddard Project
Paper supplied by Raleigh Paper
Colour reproduction by Colorific
Printed and bound by GT Graphics

Acknowledgements

The MCA would like to express sincere gratitude to Callum Morton for his time, care and commitment to the project, including his dedication in producing two major new works. We would like to thank the Guest Curator, Stuart Koop, for his work on the exhibition, and for his catalogue essay. We thank Callum's representatives, Roslyn Oxley9 Gallery, Sydney and Anna Schwartz Gallery, Melbourne; and catalogue contributor Philip Brophy. Our sincere thanks go to all lenders to the exhibition, and we acknowledge Corbett Lyon and Yueji Lyon's assistance in the production of *Habitat*.

Artist Acknowledgements

Thanks to: Jeff Binder, Andy and Ben at Bluebottle, Heather Bolton, Robin Batty at Boolean Engineering, Brian and Erin at Brian Laurence Sound, Philip Brophy, John Cherrey, Marco Ciappi, Lauren Dornau, Janeanne Eaton, Luke Elliot, Richard Giblett, Andrew S. Gilbert, Michael Goldsmith, Jackie Haliday, Trudy Hellier, Beverly and Russell 'The Rip' Hellier and Polly Hellier-Morton, Deb Hennessy, Phil at Heron Technology, Ronnie van Hout, Nick Hubicki, Stuart Koop, all the crew at Lambeth Street, Karyn Lovegrove, Corbett and Yueji Lyon, Steve Martin, Dean Boothroyd and Vivian Mitsoggiani at Matstudio, Tammy McCarthy, Modelcraft, Ian and Rhana Morton, Roslyn and Tony Oxley, Chris Reddaway, Nick Ruljanicich, Damien Salmon, Scale Models, Anna Schwartz, Russell Storer, Nick Taylor, David Tredinnick, Peter Uhd, Tim Wid, and the staff of the MCA.

Digital imaging: Nick Hubicki, Sean Elstob, Lauren Dornau, Nick Ruljanicich

All images © the artist unless otherwise specified.

▮ MUSEUM OF CONTEMPORARY ART ▮

140 George Street, The Rocks, Sydney
PO Box R1286, Sydney NSW, 1223 Australia
Phone 612 9252-4033 Fax 612 9252-4361
www.mca.com.au

Presented as part of the MCA 2003 Australian Season

 Free admission – thanks Telstra!

The Museum of Contemporary Art gratefully acknowledges the ongoing funding and support of the New South Wales Government and 'Key Organisation' grant funding from the Commonwealth Government through the Australia Council, its arts funding and advisory body. The MCA was established by the University of Sydney through the JW Power Bequest, with the assistance of the New South Wales Government.

Cover image: *Habitat* 2003
Installation view, National Gallery of Victoria Australia, Melbourne
Wood, aluminium, acrylic paint, light, sound
74 x 660 x 130 cm
Courtesy of the Corbett Lyon and Yueji Lyon Collection
Image courtesy the artist and National Gallery of Victoria
Photo: Helen Oliver-Skuse